IMAGES
of America

GREENVILLE'S
AUGUSTA ROAD

D0870432

ON THE COVER: Two Dodge trucks parked on Augusta Road are loaded up with Girl Scout cookies ready for delivery. Claussen's Bread and Cakes made over 60,000 cookies for the Girl Scouts to distribute throughout the Greenville area during their annual cookie drive. (Courtesy of the Greenville County Historical Society, Coxe Collection.)

IMAGES
of America

GREENVILLE'S AUGUSTA ROAD

Kelly Lee Odom

ARCADIA
PUBLISHING

Copyright © 2012 by Kelly Lee Odom
ISBN 978-0-7385-9187-2

Published by Arcadia Publishing
Charleston, South Carolina

Printed in the United States of America

Library of Congress Control Number: 2011944081

For all general information, please contact Arcadia Publishing:
Telephone 843-853-2070
Fax 843-853-0044
E-mail sales@arcadiapublishing.com
For customer service and orders:
Toll-Free 1-888-313-2665

Visit us on the Internet at www.arcadiapublishing.com

To all the neighbors along Augusta Road

CONTENTS

ACKNOWLEDGMENTS

With much gratitude, I thank Sidney Thompson and Jeff Willis with the Greenville County Historical Society for their resources and invaluable insight. I would also like to thank my parents, Dwight and Lee Odom, for sharing their life experiences and history in the area. Thanks also go to fellow commissioner Rick Owens for sharing his knowledge in the development of the area.

Along with the people mentioned above, the following shared valuable information: Earle Prevost; William V. McCrary Jr.; Heyward and Kay Sullivan; Joanne McCoy; Paul Ellis with the Greenville County Parks Department; Mary Johnston; Pastor Willie Thompson; Nancy Dixon of the Chanticleer Women's Club; Clarence Martin; Ruth Ann Butler; and Coy Huffman III.

The following individuals, groups, churches, schools, and organizations shared their photographs and historical archives: Susan Boyd with the South Carolina Room of the Greenville County Library; fellow commissioner Thomas Riddle; Pat Shufeldt and Westminster Presbyterian Church; Laney Stansell; Betty Stall; Roy Gullick; Jayne McCall and Hughes Development; Betty Lynn Allison; Col. Frank Foster and Rhonda Hovious with the Greenville Country Club; Kerry Bannister and Augusta Circle School; Blythe Academy; Hughes Academy; Greenville High School; Howard Leonard and St. Michael Lutheran; William T. Dunn Jr.; Charles Wofford; Judy Cromwell; Sally Roberts; Patricia Howard; Lynn Mangum and Trinity United Methodist; my brothers Scott and Chad Odom; Woo Thomason; Augusta Road Baptist Church; Beth Whitaker and the Sarah Gossett Home; Jerry Woodruff and Marshall Forest; and Debbie Roper with Augusta Heights Baptist Church. Without their contributions, this book would not have been possible.

The author has drawn upon a number of published sources. The most notable of these are Jeffrey R. Willis, *Remembering Greenville*; Sue Inman, *Growing in Faith*; Judith T. Bainbridge, *Greenville's Heritage*; John M. Nolan, *A Guide to Historic Greenville*; Henry Bacon McCoy, *Greenville, SC Facts and Memories*; Choice McCoin, *Greenville County*; Nancy Ashmore, *Greenville Woven from the Past*; Thomas Finley, *Golf in the Upstate*; and Piper Aheron, *Greenville*.

Most of all, I would like to thank my wife, Katherine, for her encouragement and technical support throughout this process; I love you.

INTRODUCTION

For many of its residents, Augusta Road is a community—a home—not just a four-lane road that takes you from Greenville to Augusta, Georgia. Technically, within the city limits, it is a street and not a road, but to newcomers and lifelong residents it will always be Augusta Road.

Augusta Road, as we know it today, runs from South Main Street to Pleasantburg Drive and is a harmonious mix of homes, shops, schools, and churches. Along its tree-lined streets are some of Greenville's oldest businesses and most prominent homes. Its name originates from the 1830s, identifying it as the trade route to Augusta.

The first suburbs of Augusta Road developed as a result of the introduction of the automobile and Greenville's lucrative textile industry. Neighborhoods such as Cagle Park, Alta Vista, and Millwood began to be developed on once sprawling farmland. As a result, schools and churches were built for these newfound residents, including the Donaldson School in 1917 and Augusta Circle in 1923.

In the years that followed, development continued southward along Augusta Road with the establishment of such neighborhoods as Cherokee Park and Kanatenah. Developer David Traxler's grand vision of a posh neighborhood built along with the Greenville Country Club's new facilities was named Traxler Park. The stone entrances to the neighborhood still stand along Augusta Road at Byrd Boulevard and Country Club Drive.

Businesses began to spring up along Augusta, including pharmacies, banks, supermarkets, and hardware stores to meet these new residents' every need. Back at the north end, construction was booming as well. In 1929, Claussen built a new state-of-the-art bakery, and in 1938, students were welcomed into the new Greenville Senior High.

Post–World War II Augusta Road saw further development of subdivisions, with neighborhoods such as Marshall Forrest and Pleasant Valley, along with the construction of churches and shopping centers. In the late 1940s, a new and exciting shopping village and apartment complex was built by real estate developer R.M. Caine, named Lewis Plaza after the family on whose property it was built. This style of shopping center was the first of its kind in the South and featured a variety of stores. Not only does the Lewis Plaza remain one of Greenville's most popular shopping destinations, it is also still managed by the Caine Company more than 60 years later.

The 1960s brought in new growth off the west side of Augusta Road with the development of Chanticleer. Brothers Robert "Red" and Jack Hughes purchased land just past Brushy Creek from the Earle family, who had a farm on the land, and planned a large, upscale neighborhood to be developed progressively in sections. Prior to being developed, the land along Brushy Creek had been used by kids growing up in Pleasant Valley for camping and hunting. Others used it for more sinister practices, such as distilling moonshine. When the Greenville Country Club was facing pressures to compete with neighboring clubs, it decided to hire world-renowned Robert Trent Jones to design an 18-hole course within the newly developed neighborhood. The course opened in 1970, and was rated one of the Top 100 golf courses in the country by *Golf Digest* in 1973.

In the years that have followed, Augusta Road has seen continuous development both commercially and residentially. The one thing that has remained constant is residents' pride in its past, making the neighborhoods, businesses, and schools along Augusta Road the most sought-after in Greenville, South Carolina.

One

EARLY DAYS

STREETCAR, AUGUSTA STREET. Pictured here around 1905, three conductors navigate the No. 4 streetcar across the Reedy River to take its passengers from Main Street to Augusta Street. The Gower, Cox, and Markley Carriage Factory can be seen just to the left of the streetcar. (Courtesy of the Greenville County Library.)

AMERICAN BANK BUILDING. In the 1870s, Dr. Thomas T. Earle opened a pharmacy on the triangular plot of land where the north end of Augusta Street ends on what is now South Main Street. Earle later went on to become president of both the Greenville County Medical Society and the South Carolina Medical Society. The pharmacy remained open until 1888, and in 1890, R.E. Allen, Henry Briggs, and Walter Gassaway organized the American Bank. The bank prospered, and as a result, Olin Jones, the same architect who had overseen the Greenville County Courthouse four years earlier, was hired to design a new Beaux-Arts building, as seen today. In 1920, the bank reorganized itself as the American Building and Loan Association with president of Judson Mill Bennette E. Geer as its president. As the West End began to decline in the late 1930s, the bank decided to close this location. In 1980, the Legal Services Agency renovated the building for its use. (Courtesy of the Greenville County Historical Society, Coxe Collection.)

ELLISON–CURETON HOUSE. Built in 1888 by Jacob Cagle for Greenville merchant Thaddeus T. Ellison, this Queen Anne home is located at the very north end of Augusta Street. Ellison had purchased the three-acre lot from Leonard Wilson for $2,500. By the time Cagle began building the house for Ellison, he had already made a name for himself, having built the Wilkins and Norwood homes. Ellison moved from Laurens, South Carolina, to open a furniture store nearby at the intersection of South Main and Augusta Streets. In 1912, Ellison sold the house to Anderson farmer James W. Dickson. Dickson's wife deeded the home to her son-in-law Peter Frank Cureton in July 1919. The residence was passed down to their daughter Josephine after their deaths, remaining in the Cureton family to this day. Built in 1858, the Greenville Hotel was located close to the home, at the corner of Augusta Street and University Ridge. The hotel was built to satisfy the needs of the West End. Families visiting Furman University students and traveling salesmen both took up stays at the hotel. (Courtesy of the Greenville County Historical Society, Coxe Collection.)

COTTONSEED OIL COMPANY. Located at the intersection of Vardy and Augusta Streets, the Cottonseed Oil Company was in operation from 1872 to 1953. It was owned and operated by Greenville businessman Otis Prentiss Mills, who also owned Augusta Road area businesses such as Millsdale Dairy and Mills Mill. In this c. 1890 photograph, several horse-drawn wagons load bales of cotton. The picket fence in the lower right corner runs alongside Vardry Street. (Courtesy of the Greenville County Library.)

COTTONSEED OIL COMPANY. In this photograph, railroad cars can be seen just below the water tank. Note that the tank reads Greenville Cotton Oil Mill Inc. The railroad tracks ran along the length of the building parallel to Augusta Street. Just above the trees on the left side of the photograph, the top story of the newly built Greenville Senior High School can be seen. (Courtesy Greenville County Historical Society, Coxe Collection.)

VIOLET HILL. This 1908 photograph shows members of the Tandy Walker family seated on the front porch. The two-story, foursquare, columned Greek Revival home was built at the north end of Augusta Street. Situated on a sloping hill, the house was later owned by the Cleveland family. It was Mary Cleveland who named the home Violet Hill. The residence later became the location of the Mary Cleveland School, and the site is now a part of Greenville High School. (Courtesy of the Greenville County Library.)

BARNET CLEVELAND HOME. The Barnet Cleveland home, also in the Greek Revival style of architecture popular in this era, was finished with four round columns and a fanlight over a six-panel front door. In this 1910 photograph, large, tropical plants and rocking chairs adorn the front porch. The homesite is currently a part of Greenville High School campus. (Courtesy of the Greenville County Library.)

O.P. MILLS RESIDENCE. A large group of children can be seen waving American flags celebrating the Fourth of July at the Mills house. Across from the Mills house was the farm of Capt. J. Westley Brooks that stood where Church Street ends at Augusta Road. After completing his home, Mills had the Brooks residence divided and reconstructed as two separate houses. One portion was moved to Mills Mill to serve as a mill superintendent's home, and the other was moved to Otis Street. (Courtesy of the Greenville County Historical Society, Landing Collection.)

MILLS MILL. Otis Prentiss Mills organized his mill in 1895, and it opened for production in 1897 with 8,000 spindles. Its mill village included a community building, school, and church. It also had an active women's club. The mill employed a full-time English gardener to landscape the mill and the surrounding village. During World War II, the mill had government contracts for war-related materials, and guards were posted around the building. Two of the guardhouses are visible in this 1940s photograph. Mills Mill was placed in the National Register of Historic Places in 1982. (Courtesy of the Greenville County Historical Society, Landing Collection.)

MILLS MILL BAPTIST CHURCH. Mill villages were established in order for mills to have a stable and constant workforce. The villages allowed workers to have affordable housing close to their employment. Along with housing, textile mill companies also established churches within the villages. Mill owners typically favored the Methodist and Baptist denominations, due to those groups' belief in a strong work ethic. Under public scrutiny and mindful of the costs associated with maintenance, mills began to sell off the homes in their villages, offering ownership to the mill workers. (Courtesy of the Greenville County Historical Society, Coxe Collection.)

MILLS MILL COMMUNITY BUILDING. In order to combat the negative connotation of the working conditions in textile mills, owners began to offer recreational activities to workers and their families. Playing fields were created, and community buildings were constructed. A community building would become the hub of the mill village and would offer a variety of activities and events. Athletic teams would meet, textile mill bands would have a place to practice, and residents would have a place for holiday activities that brought communities together. (Courtesy of the Greenville County Historical Society, Coxe Collection.)

MILLS MILL BASEBALL TEAM. From the late 1800s through the 1950s, textile league baseball was entrenched in the mill communities throughout the South. Mill owners saw the need to boost employee morale, and baseball provided the ideal outlet for both recreational and social activities. As the crowds began to grow at the games, city businesses seized the opportunity to advertise in front of a large audience. As advertising revenue grew, mill owners began to scale back the workweek in order to allow players more time to practice. It became a moneymaking opportunity for mill owners, and teams began bidding for players to stay competitive. There were rules as to who could play textile league baseball. The most important rule was that players had to work for the mill. By the 1930s, player's pay tended to be 10 to 20 times higher than that of the average mill worker. The 1950s began to see a decline in textile league ball for a variety of reasons. The primary factor was that mill owners sold off the homes in their villages, eliminating community bonds. Also, as television became mainstream, attendance at games began to drop. By the early 1970s, textile league baseball had disappeared. (Courtesy of the Greenville County Historical Society, Coxe Collection.)

THRUSTON HOUSE. Located at 506 Augusta Street, this two-story, brick structure with a wooden front porch was built for Thomas Barksdale and Annie Bush Thruston. Note the woman standing in the garden with a dog on the right of the photograph above. The garden included a large number of boxwoods and yellow jonquils. The first floor of the home consisted of a parlor, sitting room, dining room, and plunder room, later turned into a kitchen once it was moved inside the home. The second floor was made up of four bedrooms and a covered porch on the rear, which was later converted into an apartment for rent. The second floor exterior was later covered in white clapboard siding as seen in the photograph below. A portion of the property became the site of the Greenville Baseball Park in 1925, and later, the Graham Athletic Field, Furman's baseball stadium. Other prominent residents along Augusta Street at the time included H.C. Markley, owner of the Markley Carriage Factory; J.M. Sullivan, owner of Sullivan Hardware; J.O. Bailey, editor of *The Mountaineer and Enterprise*; and H.P. Hammett, president of the Piedmont Mill. The Thruston home was demolished in 1967. (Above, courtesy of the Greenville County Library; below, courtesy of the Greenville County Historical Society, Landing Collection.)

T.Q. DONALDSON HOUSE. Located at 412 Crescent Avenue, the Donaldson house was built in 1863 as the private residence for William Williams, professor at the Baptist Theological Seminary. Designed in the Italianate style, the home was originally constructed as a 1.5-story cottage, but soon after completion, the second story was added. In 1867, the home was acquired by Squire T.Q. Donaldson, a prominent lawyer and a member of the South Carolina Senate from 1872 to 1876. The home was placed in the National Register of Historic Places in September 1980. (Courtesy of the Greenville County Historical Society, Landing Collection.)

J.C. MILFORD HOME. Located at 706 Augusta Street, the Milford home was the third on the right after passing Dunbar Street heading south. The brick structure included a slate roof, stone porte cochere, covered front porch, and chimney. During the 1860s, other prominent Greenvillians, including Greenville's first physician, Dr. Richard Harrison, built homes around Depot Green, the name for the area surrounding the Greenville and Columbia Railroad Depot, built in 1853. (Courtesy of the Greenville County Historical Society, Landing Collection.)

MILTON SMITH HOME. Located at 1201 Augusta Street at the southeast corner of Augusta and then Crescent Avenue, the Milton Smith home was purchased out of the Sears, Roebuck and Co. catalog. Once purchased, the home package would be sent to the building site ready to be assembled. Other Sears homes in the Augusta Road area are located on McDaniel Avenue and Rice Street. Before Church Street was extended to Augusta in 1955, Crescent Avenue ran from Augusta Road all the way to McDaniel Farm. (Courtesy of the Greenville County Historical Society, Landing Collection.)

CAGLE HOUSE. Originally the Earle farmhouse, this house was purchased by Jacob Cagle along with its 39 acres in 1882. Cagle was known for building the Wilkins house on Augusta Road and the Lanneau–Norwood house. In 1979, Cagle designed the short-lived Greenville Opera House, located on the corner of South Main Street and McBee Avenue. Just three months after completion, the opera house was destroyed by fire. (Courtesy of the Greenville County Historical Society, Landing Collection.)

BIRNIE HILL. This house was built in 1847 by Professor Kern on Augusta Road at the location of present-day Lewis Plaza shopping center. In 1861, the property was sold to James Birnie, whose daughter married local druggist J.O. Lewis. Lewis was an equestrian and had a large stable constructed on the property full of horses to fuel his passion. It was the Lewis family who named the home Birnie Hill. A large, covered porch, draped with vines, spans the entire front facade. (Courtesy of the Greenville County Historical Society, Landing Collection.)

BIRNIE HILL. The home was later moved to its present location on Aberdeen Drive, where it still stands today. The large porch has been removed and a small, pillared awning was added. The structure was converted into an apartment house and is still in use today. (Courtesy of the Greenville County Historical Society, Landing Collection.)

FARIS ROAD AT AUGUSTA ROAD. Looking south from Faris Road, this 1920s photograph shows a very rural Augusta Road. Wide-open fields and the David Elwood McCuen home can be seen where a McDonald's and a shopping center with Firehouse Subs and Alpine Ski Center can be seen today. Augusta Road was only a smooth dirt road at the time. (Courtesy of Woo McCuen Thomason.)

THE PICKWICK SANDWICH SHOP. Seeing the opportunity to purchase a large tract of land out in the country on Augusta Road, father and son Archibald Clinch and Francis Odom moved their sandwich shop from their West End, Augusta Road location to the new rural site. Construction of the new sandwich shop cost $1,200, and work was to be completed in two weeks. Augusta Road, with its dirt roadbed, can be seen in the forefront. With the automobile becoming more commonplace, Augusta Road's dirt lanes were less than adequate. In 1909, an automobile traveling without incident from Bamberg to Greenville (24 hours of steady driving) broke its front spring when it entered Greenville on Augusta Road. Residents petitioned city council to improve the roadbed, and in 1913, the street was paved in concrete to Grove Road. Improvements to the road came with time, and in 1925, the road was macadamized out to McDaniel Avenue. By 1927, Augusta Road had been designated US Highway 25, allowing it to have a hard surface paved along the roadbed. (Courtesy of the author.)

So Big. As the effects of the Great Depression subsided, more funding became available to the Greenville County Library system, allowing more service in the branches. A new branch was opened on Augusta Street on a lot owned by L.O. Patterson. Probably the smallest branch constructed in the country, it was aptly called "So Big." Built at a cost of $24.50, excluding labor provided by the Works Progress Administration, it was six feet by four and a half feet wide and seven feet tall. Inside the building were 42 feet of shelving and a built-in desk and folding chair. The bookmobile, named "the Pathfinder," full of books being delivered to the branches, is parked next to So Big, while a line of children waits to check out books. (Courtesy of the Greenville County Library.)

Greenville Columbia Depot. Seen here with the Butler Guard, the Greenville Columbia train depot was a bustling center during the Civil War. Presbyterian minister E.T. Buist would read aloud the names of the dead and wounded from the station platform while pine coffins lay nearby waiting for families to claim their departed loved ones. (Courtesy of Don Koonce.)

Two

BUSINESS CORRIDOR

ASIA RUG COMPANY. Owned by Charles E. Saad, the Asia Rug Company handled the sales, cleaning, and storage of Oriental rugs. With members of the Saad family as employees, the company prospered and remained the only Oriental rug store in Greenville for many years. Other small businesses opened in the area during the 1940s, including the Lucky Strike Café, the Dixie Grille, and the Clean Cleaners. Seen here at their newly built Augusta Street location are Mr. and Mrs. Charles Saad, along with two unidentified individuals standing behind them. Many pieces of Asian art and figurines that are for sale are neatly displayed in the windows. In later years, the Asia Rug Company relocated to Main Street. (Courtesy of the Greenville County Historical Society, Coxe Collection.)

FURMAN UNIVERSITY PEP RALLY. Students, joined hand-in-hand during a Furman University pep rally, walk up University Ridge to Augusta Street. The building to the left was the Pickwick Sandwich Shop, a popular gathering place for college students at the time. The Pickwick received its name from the Charles Dickens novel *The Pickwick Papers*, in which students often gathered at the Pickwick Pub. The sandwich shop's menu is painted on the side of the building. The structure is currently the home of the Warehouse Theatre. (Courtesy of the author.)

FARMERS' ALLIANCE COTTON WAREHOUSE. In 1890, preeminent Greenville builder Jacob Cagle was hired to build a cotton warehouse at the corner of South Main and Augusta Streets for the Farmers' Alliance. At the time, Greenville's textile industry was booming and Greenville County was producing nearly 30,000 bales of cotton per year, so a central warehouse was needed. The Farmers' Alliance came into being as a result of post–Civil War farmers needing to band together for economic survival. The alliance organized in Greenville in the 1880s, and 42 regional alliances came together to build the warehouse in order to cut out the commodity brokers, thus boosting their profits. (Courtesy of the Greenville County Historical Society, Coxe Collection.)

HERNDON'S ESSO STATION. Located at the intersection of South Main and Augusta Streets, Herndon's Esso Service Station was in the heart of Greenville's first motor mile. Tire Centers, service stations, and automobile dealerships for brands such as Ford, Cadillac, and Mercury—seen here to the left of the service station—were all clustered in the West End, along South Main and Augusta Streets. Cans of motor oil and tires are neatly stacked about the station, and signs advertising 24-hour service and gas for $0.189 per gallon are visible. (Courtesy of the Greenville County Historical Society, Coxe Collection.)

COLLINS MOTOR COMPANY. The gleaming showroom floor sets the perfect backdrop to display the newest models of the Cadillac line. Nicely dressed salesmen flank the new cars, while fresh bouquets of flowers and plants adorn the spotless showroom. Located at the north end of Augusta Street, Collins Motor Company was in the middle of Greenville's first motor mile. Many other

automobile dealerships and automotive-related businesses opened up in the West End as a result of the automobile becoming more attainable for the average citizen. (Courtesy of the Greenville County Historical Society, Coxe Collection.)

Motor Mile. As the automobile became more accessible and affordable, Greenville quickly met the consumers' needs. At the north end of Augusta Road, service stations, auto supply stores, and new and used car dealerships lined the street. Seen here are the Richfield service station, A-1 Used Cars and Trucks, the Economy service station, Collins Cadillac, the Ford dealership, M and J Finance Corporation, and the Smith Coal Company. The Smith Coal Company's billboards clever slogans reads, "Smith Coal Answers the Burning Question" and "Sho Am Hot Stuf." The Smith Coal location later became the site of a Pabst Blue Ribbon distributor and then the Greenville Transit Authority. (Courtesy of the Greenville County Historical Society, Coxe Collection.)

CLAUSSEN'S BAKERY. Located at 400 Augusta Street, Claussen's Bread and Cakes bakery was built in 1930 for the sum of $200,000. The two-story, 42,000-square-foot, triangular building is sitting on 2.5 acres. It was built as a replica to its sister plant in Columbia. The aromas of breads, cookies, and cake, baked daily, welcomed students at Greenville High School as well as passersby. (Courtesy of the Greenville County Historical Society, Coxe Collection.)

CLAUSSEN'S BAKERY DELIVERY TEAM. Claussen's Bread and Cakes bakery was located alongside the railroad tracks that follow Augusta Street to the West End. Claussen's supplied baked goods to most of the grocery stores in the county. In order to accomplish this task, the bakery required a fleet of delivery trucks, which are proudly displayed in this photograph. Painted on the side of the delivery trucks is the company slogan, "Claussen's Bread for Extra Energy." (Courtesy of the Greenville County Historical Society, Coxe Collection.)

THE MARKET BASKET. Located at the corner of Augusta and Sullivan Streets, the Market Basket, later the Marquette, was the local butcher shop that supplied meats to residents along Augusta Road, as well as to restaurants and soda shops. Owned and operated by Buddy and Louise Ray, the Market Basket would make deliveries and extend charge accounts to its customers. Seen in the storefront window is an elaborate apple display with the letters of their vendor, Skookum, strung across it. (Courtesy of the Greenville County Historical Society, Coxe Collection.)

DEAN BROTHERS. Located at the corner of Otis and Augusta Streets, Dean Brothers' Shell service station, later Miller Oil Company, offered full-service attention to its customers. Seen here, the service station is well decorated for the holidays, with snowflakes and Santa Claus in the window and a decorated tree and bells above the awning. (Courtesy of the Greenville County Historical Society, Coxe Collection.)

SPANISH MOTOR COURT. Positioned at the corner of Augusta and Grove Roads, the Spanish Motor Court was owned by Greenville Senior High School's assistant junior varsity football coach Mr. Hillhouse. This postcard was a memento visitors could use to correspond to their families back home. (Courtesy of the author.)

BORDER'S GULF STATION. Located at the corner of Cleveland Street and University Ridge across from Sirrine Stadium, Border's Gulf still operates as a full-service gasoline station. The building has been unaltered in its 70-plus years in business. The Woodside Building and a horse-drawn buggy can be seen in the distance to the right of the power lines. (Courtesy of the Greenville County Historical Society, Coxe Collection.)

TUTEN-MART. Located at the corner of University Ridge and Cleveland Street, the Tuten-Mart was developed by the Ralph O. Tuten Realty Company in 1946. The building was comprised of a luncheonette featuring Hostess Ice Cream, the University Beauty Shop, and a drugstore. The left side of the shopping center was occupied by a Piggly Wiggly grocery store and was later home to the Eight O'clock Superette. The building was razed in the 1970s to make way for a new structure for the Eight O'clock Superette. (Courtesy of the Greenville County Historical Society, Coxe Collection.)

MIKE SIEGEL'S ESSO STATION. Located in the Tuten-Mart parking lot at the corner of University Ridge and Cleveland Street was Siegel's Esso Station. Along with Siegel's, two other gasoline stations occupied the corners of this small intersection—the Texaco Oil Company and Border's Gulf Station. Visible through the service bay are the University Ridge Apartments. To the right of the service station is the Piggly Wiggly. (Courtesy of the Greenville County Historical Society, Coxe Collection.)

SARAH SIMPSON GOSSETT RETIREMENT HOME. Opening in 1909 as the Ingleside Association on the corner of McBee Avenue and Westfield Street, it was organized by a group of women led by Mamie McEachern, who saw a need for economical housing for young, professional women. When the YWCA began to offer similar boarding in the late 1910s, the Ingleside Association shifted its focus to accommodate seniors. On November 11, 1937, Ingleside reopened in a building owned by the D.D. Davenport estate at 536 West Washington Street, and the home and governing association were renamed after Martha Davenport. With the Washington Street facility becoming less conducive for its purpose, the association sought a new location and found five lots on Conestee Avenue available for purchase at a cost of $10,150. As fundraising efforts began, naming rights were offered to the first donor offering a gift of $25,000. Ralph Gossett was that donor. He wished to have the building named in memory of his wife, Sarah Simpson, who had been an avid supporter of the Davenport Home. In fact, her last day was spent gathering flowers on Paris Mountain to place around the home. The new Sarah Simpson Gossett Retirement home, designed by architect W.E. Freeman, would hold 30 residents; landscaping was contributed by local garden clubs. Residents were able to move in to the new location in December 1955. (Courtesy of the Greenville County Historical Society, Coxe Collection.)

LEWIS PLAZA. While stationed in California during World War II, developer R.M. Caine came across a new style of shopping center never before seen in the South. After his time in service, Caine came back to Greenville and built this new concept in the heart of Augusta Street. Named for the Lewis family, whose home once stood on the land, the Lewis Plaza was the first of its kind in the South. Over 50 years later, it is still managed by the Caine Company. (Courtesy of the Greenville County Historical Society, Elrod Collection.)

LEWIS PLAZA. Instantly becoming a shopping destination, the Lewis Plaza was comprised of a variety of establishments catering to various consumer needs. Storefronts of the Plaza Pharmacy, Suttons Shoes, Crane's, Scott and Merritt, Bihari's Delicatessen, and Rose's Five-and-Ten can be seen. The *Flying Leatherheads*, starring John Wayne, is playing at the Plaza Theater. (Courtesy of the Greenville County Historical Society, Coxe Collection.)

No. 3 Fire Station. The Greenville Fire Department built its Augusta Road branch at the corner of Faris and Augusta Roads. Glass doors and a much larger parking area extending out to both Augusta and Faris Roads can be seen. Signage for the fire department above the front door entrance was added at a later date. (Courtesy of the Greenville County Historical Society, Elrod Collection.)

FIRST FEDERAL SAVINGS AND LOAN. The First Federal Savings and Loan was located at the corner of Augusta Street and Augusta Drive. The name Augusta is used for seven different types of road designations in the area including circle, court, drive, place, road, street, and terrace. Within the city limits, Augusta is a street. It is not until the city line at the intersection of Mauldin and Augusta Roads that it officially takes on the name *road*. (Courtesy of the Greenville County Historical Society, Coxe Collection.)

TRAVELING CIRCUS. During the 1940s, traveling circuses would put up their big tops on the driving range at the corner of Augusta Road and Potomac Avenue. The circus would typically feature a variety of wild animals and sideshow acts. Seen here are camels grazing in the driving range, with the homes along Potomac Avenue in the distance. (Courtesy of the author.)

CIRCUS ELEPHANTS. Traveling circuses would parade down Augusta to entice residents to come to the shows. Seen here are elephants walking and holding trunk to tail in front of Slater's Cash Grocery, once located at the corner of Augusta Road and Wilmont Lane. (Courtesy of the author.)

PICKWICK SANDWICH SHOP. After serving in World War II, brothers Francis and Edgar Odom returned home to reopen their sandwich shop on Augusta Road, this time adding a pharmacy. The octagonal entrance was added in 1947, with signs from vendors, such as the Merita Bread, hung on the screen door. Along with the expansion, carhops and drive-in service were added to the sandwich shop. (Courtesy of the author.)

PICKWICK PHARMACY. In 1949, a brick facade was added to the front and side of Pickwick Pharmacy. Coca-Cola advertisements, button-style signs, and awnings are indicative of the era. Parked out front are 1949 and 1947 Chevrolets. (Courtesy of the author.)

EDGAR ODOM. Behind the pharmacy counter, Pickwick's pharmacist Edgar Odom is counting pills. This photograph was taken for an article in the *Piedmont Paper* on Odom's life and business. Odom was entrenched in the southern end of the Augusta Road community, operating a business, residing on Crystal Avenue, and helping to establish Augusta Heights Baptist Church. (Courtesy of author.)

PICKWICK SHOPPING CENTER. With rapid growth in residential development along Augusta Road, the need for consumer goods and services was on the rise. To meet these needs, shopping centers were built, such as the Pickwick Shopping Center. The S.C. Rush Barber Shop and Pickwick Pharmacy can be seen in the building closer to the street, while the new shopping center is being constructed in the rear. Occupying the shopping center in the forefront were the Fluff and Dry Laundrymat, Circle D Market, and the School of Dance. (Courtesy of the author.)

PICKWICK SHOPPING CENTER. This 1958 photograph shows a completed shopping center with an array of tenants meeting the consumer's needs. The storefronts of Gregory's Cleaners, Pickwick Toys and Hobbies, the Pickwick Pharmacy, Barber Service, and Emery Five and Dime can be seen. Not pictured to the far left of the center was Dixie Hardware. Pic 'n' Pay shoe store can be seen in the next shopping center over. (Courtesy of the author.)

AUGUSTA ROAD ANIMAL HOSPITAL. Will T. Dunn, DVM, purchased 6.5 acres of land on the south end of Augusta Road and built his veterinary clinic and family residence on the property. The clinic opened in 1946. (Courtesy of Will T. Dunn Jr.)

VETERINARY CLINIC. Designed by Doctor Dunn, the state-of-the-art building was escape-proof and vermin-proof. It was constructed solely of concrete and steel and was equipped with radiant heat pipes underneath the floor and cooled by a sprinkler system on the roof, in order to keep the animals from getting sick from conventional air-conditioning. Seen here, from left to right, are Dr. William Dunn, Mr. and Mrs. C.M. Wing, Will T. Dunn Jr., and Lucia Dunn. The Wings loaned Dr. Dunn the funds to purchase and construct his hospital. (Courtesy of Will T. Dunn Jr.)

WILLIAM TILLMAN DUNN, DVM. Having graduated from the Ohio State University College of Veterinary Medicine, Dr. Dunn came to Greenville after briefly practicing in Hartsville, where he met his wife, Lucia. He practiced from 1936 until his death in 2000, making him the longest-practicing veterinarian in the state. (Courtesy of Will T. Dunn Jr.)

PAYNE BROTHERS DAIRY. Payne's bottling operation was located directly on Augusta Road, while its dairy farm was located outside of town. Its assembly line was fully automated, and tours were given to local elementary school students. When Augusta Heights Baptist Church was first being organized, the congregation was allowed to meet at the dairy while awaiting construction across the street. The bottling plant closed in 1954. (Courtesy of Augusta Heights Baptist Church.)

AUGUSTA ROAD CORRIDOR. This aerial photograph was taken by Greenville photographer William B. Coxe. Born in Sanford, North Carolina, Coxe came to Greenville after World War I and immediately established himself as a photographer, keeping a studio on the top floor of the Woodside Building. He began to chronicle the growth and development of Greenville through the use of photography and dedicated the next 55 years of his life to doing so. To complement his own collection, he purchased the collections of both James Huntington and William Preston Dowling, dating back to 1900. Bill Coxe was both a professional and personal photographer, taking photos of individuals, events, organizations, buildings, churches, and private residences. He was the official photographer of the Southern Textile Exhibition and shot portraits of individuals, including the likes of Howard Hughes and Charles Lindbergh. In order for Coxe to obtain the aerial angles he wanted, which most pilots would not fly, he got his own pilot's license. His civic contributions included serving as president of both the Kiwanis Club and Greenville Art Association. During his career, Coxe amassed over 120,000 negatives of film, not including the collections he purchased. Coxe died in 1973 at the age of 78. (Courtesy of Hughes Development.)

Three

NEIGHBORHOODS AND PARKS

HORSEBACK. David Elwood "Shorty" McCuen Jr. is riding Pink at the corner of Augusta and Grove Roads in the early 1920s, when this section of Augusta Road was residential. McCuen was raised in a house his parents built at the corner of Faris and Augusta Roads. After marrying, he and Eugenia Poe Cogswell built a home on Augusta Road near St. Michael Lutheran Church. Augusta Road was paved in concrete from Main Street to this corner and was not extended beyond Grove Road until the late 1920s. (Courtesy of Woo McCuen Thomason.)

WOFFORD HOUSE. The Wofford house was built in the 1920s at the corner of West Prentiss and Augusta Streets by Greenville attorney Tom Wofford and his wife, Caro; they raised five children there. This intersection of Augusta Road was the end of the trolley line, so the homesite had to be set at an angle to allow trolleys to turn around. This house and two others that made up the block between West Prentiss and Mills Avenues were demolished in 1974 to make way for a commercial project. (Courtesy of the Wofford family.)

PIERCE THOMPSON HOUSE. This home was once located on Augusta Street. The site is now the location of the YWCA. Pierce Thompson worked as a header in a cotton mill at the age of 12. He went on to open Eagle Iron Works, a metal foundry and machine shop located at 401 Dunbar Street. (Courtesy of the Greenville County Historical Society, Coxe Collection.)

AUGUSTA STREET HOUSE. Located at the corner of East Prentiss and Augusta Street, the three-story, wood clapboard home was built in the Federal style. The home is marked by a symmetrical pattern of double-hung windows, arranged about a central front door with an ornamental surround, sidelights, and a paneled fanlight. Elaborate balustrades line the roofs of the projected wings. (Courtesy of the Greenville County Historical Society, Coxe Collection.)

SPANISH HOUSE. Located opposite where Grove Road ends, this Spanish-style home was built with stucco walls and terra-cotta roof. Seated on the steps at the street are a babysitter, two children, and an infant. The yard is well landscaped with a border of English boxwoods. A concrete Augusta Street can be seen. (Courtesy of the Greenville County Historical Society, Coxe Collection.)

HARRIS HOME. This home was built in 1908 by noted architect Frank H. Cunningham, of Cunningham and Cunningham, for Harry H. and Janie Harris at a price of $7,000. The Harris home shows the influence of the Tudor style, popular in the first part of the 20th century. Cunningham graduated Clemson College with a degree in textile engineering. After graduation, he worked as a textile engineer for Joseph E. Sirrine before partnering with his own brother Frank. The brothers began the architectural firm Cunningham and Cunningham in 1908. Frank passed away in 1928 at the age of 48. (Courtesy of the Greenville County Historical Society, Coxe Collection.)

PRIDEMORE RESIDENCE. The Pridemore residence was located on Crescent Avenue across from the Harry H. Harris home. Crescent Avenue was first built by Greenville builder Jacob Cagle in the 1890s as a part of his new development, Crescent Ridge Spa, which was created around a mineral spring on modern-day Capers Street. Cagle advertised his new neighborhood as "a fine place to raise chickens and children." (Courtesy of the Greenville County Historical Society, Coxe Collection.)

CAGLE HOUSE. This is the Cagle house as it appears today on Crescent Avenue. The home was originally situated facing Augusta Street, but in 1926, it was renovated and moved to face Crescent Avenue as Cagle's son Jacob began to develop Cagle Park. Nearby Eagle Avenue was originally named Cagle. The road was incorrectly recorded as Eagle in city documents, and the name Eagle remained. (Courtesy Greenville County Historical Society, Landing Collection.)

WOODSIDE HOUSE. The Woodside house was designed by William "Willie" Ward for textile magnate John T. Woodside and his wife, Lucille. Along with his textile business, Woodside would go on to build the Woodside Building on Main Street and to develop the opulent Ocean Forest Hotel in Myrtle Beach. Unfortunately, the stock market crash of 1929 would take most of Woodside's holdings, forcing him to move from the home. During a renovation of the home in 1947, the house caught fire and was made into a one-story home. In 2003, the home was restored to its original design. (Courtesy of the Greenville County Historical Society, Coxe Collection.)

PEACE RESIDENCE. Roger Craft and Laura Estelle Chandler Peace resided at this home, designed by Willie Ward for Dr. J.W. Jervey and located at 201 Crescent Avenue. Roger was born on May 19, 1899, and was the son of Bony Hampton Peace. After serving in World War I, he went on to attend Furman University. After graduation, he and his brother urged their father to purchase the *Greenville News*, which had been struggling financially at the time. Roger went to work for the paper as the sports editor and rose through the ranks to become publisher and president in 1934. In 1941, he was named by Gov. Burnet R. Maybank to fill a four-month interim-term US senate seat vacated by James F. Byrnes when he was appointed to the US Supreme Court by President Roosevelt. Roger was named to both the South Carolina Press and the South Carolina Business Halls of Fame. He also served on the boards of several companies including the People's National Bank of Greenville, Piedmont and Northern Railway, and the Greenville Community Hotel Corporation. (Courtesy of the Greenville County Historical Society, Coxe Collection.)

CAGLE PARK. A partially developed neighborhood can be seen in this aerial photograph. The intersection of Capers Street and Crescent Avenue is just above the center, and the lavish gardens and home of Roger C. Peace are on the left. The Woodside house, before it was destroyed by fire, is in the center, with Lupo Street running behind. East Prentiss, Jones, and Tindal Avenues frame the photograph. At the time, many vacant lots remain in what is today a densely populated area. (Courtesy of the Greenville County Historical Society, Coxe Collection.)

NEWTON HOUSE. Located at the corner of McDaniel and Crescent Avenues, the white clapboard Newton home was designed by famed Greenville architect William "Willie" Ward. Large brick pillars once stood at the intersection to mark the entrance for Alta Vista. These brick pillars were later removed. (Courtesy of the Greenville County Historical Society, Coxe Collection.)

415 CRESCENT AVENUE. Built for Charlie Daniel, owner of Daniel Construction Company, this home features a facade made of brick that was left over from a project of Daniel's. A building originally constructed as a separate living quarters for staff was later attached to the right side of the home during a renovation. Other prominent Greenvillians who have resided in the home include federal judge Clement F. Haynsworth and the Buck Mickel family. (Courtesy of the Greenville County Historical Society, Coxe Collection.)

DAVIS RESIDENCE. This French Provincial home, located at the corner of Crescent and McDaniel Avenues, was designed for Thomas Gordon and Janette McPherson Davis. A banker at Peoples National, Davis had the home built in 1931. Due to the Great Depression, it was one of only two building contracts in Greenville. Family members say the Davises kept a pony in the basement. The home has remained in the family to this day. (Courtesy of the Greenville County Historical Society, Coxe Collection.)

FOURTH OF JULY. Families are getting prepared for the annual Fourth of July parade on Lanneau Drive. The street is built on what was once the site of Charles H. Lanneau's textile mill, which covered the property between Lanneau and Camille Avenues. (Courtesy of Patricia W. Howard.)

S STORE FIRE ENGINE. The S Store fire engine led the annual Fourth of July parade in Alta Vista. The slogan written down the side of the engine reads, "Prices are so hot, the S Store had to buy a fire truck." The fire engine made appearances at various events and functions throughout the year, including the Christmas parade on Main Street. (Courtesy of Patricia W. Howard.)

ROBINSON RESIDENCE. This one-story, cedar-shake home was built for the J.V. Robinson family on one of the largest lots in Alta Vista. To the left of the residence, snow-covered houses on nearby Lanneau Drive are visible, and wide-open fields can be seen beyond the home on the right. (Courtesy of the Greenville County Historical Society, Coxe Collection.)

MCDANIEL AVENUE. McDaniel Avenue was first drawn out in 1863 by Furman professor Basil Manly as a path leading from Augusta Road to "Widow McDaniel's farm." Manly had just purchased 25 acres of land from the estate of John Coleman in hopes of subdividing and selling the property to his fellow university professors. (Courtesy of the Greenville County Historical Society, Coxe Collection.)

JOHNSTON RESIDENCE. The Johnson residence was built in 1936 for Woodside Cotton Mills chairman Ellis M. and wife, Julliette, Johnston, at a staggering price of $29,000. The home was designed by William "Willie" Ward, who is considered one of South Carolina's most noted architects of the 20th century. Born in Eutaw, Alabama, in 1890, Ward skipped high school and entered Auburn University. He began his career as a draftsman for the New York firm Hill and South while attending night classes at Columbia University to obtain his master's in architecture. During his time in New York, he met Greenville native Haskell Martin, who proposed forming a partnership back in South Carolina. Ward was later stationed in Paris during World War I. While in Paris, he attended classes at the École des Beaux-Arts, furthering his education and influencing his later design work. After being released from service, he traveled directly to Greenville to join Martin and begin his career. Ward designed homes, churches, and some commercial buildings until his retirement in 1957. After retirement, he returned home to Alabama, where he died in 1984 at the age of 94. In all, Ward has built 133 structures, including several homes he designed in the Alta Vista neighborhood. (Courtesy of the Greenville County Historical Society, Coxe Collection.)

ALDEN SIMPSON HOUSE. Located at the corner of McDaniel Avenue and Newman Street, this home was built in the 1930s on the site of the William B. McDaniel home. The McDaniel home was originally built on Paris Mountain by congressman and diplomat Waddy Thompson Jr. The home is said to have been constructed without nails, thus allowing the house to be moved to its Greenville location in 1866. McDaniel lived in the home until his death in 1928, and the structure was demolished in 1934. Newman Street was created after the house was razed and was named for McDaniel's daughter Annie Lou McDaniel Newman. (Courtesy of the Greenville County Historical Society, Coxe Collection.)

CLEVELAND STREET AT MCDANIEL AVENUE. A sparsely developed neighborhood can be seen in this aerial photograph. Land to the left of McDaniel Avenue is terraced, while no streets have been cut to the north of Cleveland Street, including Newman and Ben Streets. Belmont Avenue abruptly ends behind the Johnston home, seen in the center. Note that the great oaks that line the streets today are mere saplings at this time. (Courtesy of the Greenville County Historical Society, Coxe Collection.)

CLEVELAND STREET. Brick homes neatly line the first residential block of Cleveland Street. Residents of this block are privileged with a secret park behind their homes. (Courtesy of the Greenville County Historical Society, Coxe Collection.)

JUDSON HOME. In 1863, Furman University professor Charles Judson purchased 17 acres of land from the Coleman estate and built this Victorian home. The house originally faced McDaniel, but was later moved to its present location on Cleveland Street. Judson Mill and its village were named in honor of Charles Judson. (Courtesy of the author.)

CLEVELAND PARK SWIMMING POOL. In 1939, a swimming pool and skating rink were added to Cleveland Park. During integration, the pool was closed in 1964, and a seal exhibit was opened in its place. Later, a rose garden replaced the seal exhibit, and then in 1988, the rose garden and skating rink were removed to make way for the present-day tennis courts. (Both, courtesy of the Greenville of the Greenville County Historical Society, Coxe Collection.)

MAJ. RUDOLF ANDERSON MEMORIAL. An F-86 Sabre airplane is displayed by the Reedy River in Cleveland Park to memorialize Greenville native Maj. Rudolf Anderson. He was a pilot in the US Air Force and was the first recipient of the Air Force Cross. Anderson was killed when his aircraft was shot down while flying over Cuban airspace during the Cuban Missile Crisis. (Courtesy of the Greenville County Historical Society, Coxe Collection.)

CLEVELAND PARK. In December 1924, William Choice Cleveland donated 112 acres of land along the Reedy River to the city, creating Cleveland Park. The park would complement his new housing development, Cleveland Forest, and would be an equestrian park including paddocks and stables. Residents of the new neighborhood could board their horses close to home. A fire that broke out in the paddocks in the 1940s would end its equestrian focus. (Courtesy of the Greenville County Historical Society, Coxe Collection.)

CLEVELAND PARK BRIDGE. Workers build a massive stone bridge to allow East Washington Street to overpass Richland Way and Richland Creek. For fun, many Greenville residents sound their horns as they drive through the one-car-wide tunnel. (Courtesy of the Greenville County Historical Society, Coxe Collection.)

CLEVELAND PARK. The City of Greenville had originally planned to dam up the Reedy River in order to create a lake in the middle of the park. This plan never came to fruition, but under the Works Progress Administration, the river was channelized in order to make recreation areas in the park. (Courtesy of the Greenville County Historical Society, Coxe Collection.)

ROCK QUARRY GARDEN. The Rock Quarry Garden, once the site of a Civil War granite quarry, is located along McDaniel Avenue just above Cleveland Park. In 1928, the newly formed Greenville Garden Club, led by Mrs. H.T. Crigler, felt the city of Greenville needed an arboretum. To raise funds for the arboretum, members of the garden club approached city officials with an "out of the box" idea to beautify the abandoned rock quarry and to submit the project to the *Better Homes and Gardens* 1931 city beautification contest. Their argument was that even if they lost, the city would still end up with a beautiful, new public garden. Officials agreed, and landscape architect Carter Newman designed the new park. Photographer William Coxe took photographs for the submission. The garden club won second place and enough money to build the arboretum at Reedy River Falls. The arboretum is now gone, but the Rock Quarry Garden remains a horticultural wonder and a favorite location for weddings and portraits. (Courtesy of the author.)

ALLEN JOHNSON HOME. Located at 12 Woodland Way Circle, the large, two-story, brick Allen Johnson home was built in 1937 with a tile roof. Seven years after Cleveland Park was established, Woodland Way Circle was completed but was first called Choice Avenue after its developer, William Choice Cleveland. (Courtesy of the Greenville County Historical Society, Coxe Collection.)

TROOP 19. The local Boy Scout Troop 19 was located in a log cabin on Brookwood Drive. Pictured in January 31, 1951, a group of Boy Scouts stands in front of an eight-man-perimeter tent. The cabin can be seen behind the tent, as can houses facing Melville Avenue. (Courtesy of Roy Gullick.)

MCCUEN RESIDENCE. The David Elwood McCuen house appears as it did when it was built in the 1920s on Augusta Road. The home and its property encompassed most of the block between Faris Road and Augusta Drive and included gardens, a tennis court, and large walnut trees that framed the front of the house. Mrs. McCuen was an avid gardener and active in the Greenville Garden Club. She was also responsible for helping create Rock Quarry Garden on McDaniel Avenue. The house was torn down after her death in 1962 and the site developed into the shopping center visible today. Many of the home's architectural elements found new life in the construction of a house off Parkins Mill Road. (Courtesy of Woo McCuen Thomason.)

HATCH HOME. Chester Elbert and Maybelle Hatch purchased the property located at the corner of McDaniel Avenue and Augusta Road in 1915 to build their New England–style home and barn. Maybelle was an avid gardener, and many weddings were held under her rose arbors. In 1918, the Hatches planted a magnolia tree that has grown to be the enormous landmark seen today. (Courtesy of Sally Hatch Roberts.)

LONGVIEW TERRACE. A newly developed Longview Terrace can be seen, with vacant lots and a dirt road without curbing. The three homes on the left have similar floor plans with minor differences. (Courtesy of the Greenville County Historical Society, Coxe Collection.)

TRAXLER REAL ESTATE COMPANY. The 1911 sales force for the Traxler Real Estate Company was responsible for developing the Traxler Park neighborhood, situated beside the Greenville Country Club. Members of the sales force include Mr. Turner, Mr. Bradley, Stames Spellmeyer, D.H. Traxler, D.B. Traxler, and Mason Ballenger. (Courtesy of the Greenville County Public Library.)

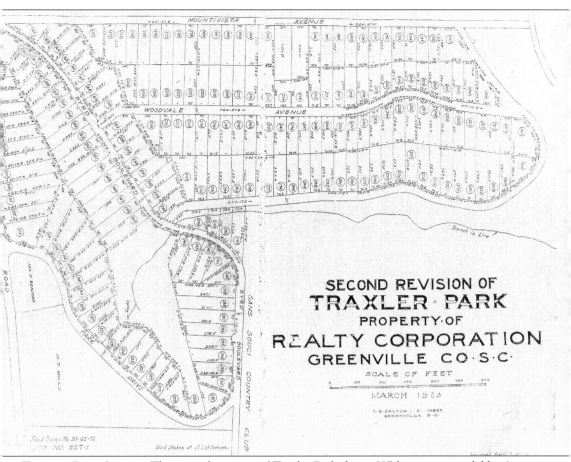

Traxler Park Survey. The second revision of Traxler Park shows 297 homesites available. At the time of the survey, Rock Creek Drive had not been named, and Country Club Drive was named Park Drive. Walls of stonework were erected at both entrances intersecting Augusta Road to mark the neighborhood. (Courtesy of Howard Leonard.)

THE BRIAR PATCH. Named for the briar patch area of Byrd Boulevard on which it was built, the home of Bony Hampton Peace Jr. was designed by architect Henry Ivan Gaines of Asheville, North Carolina. At the time it was built, Byrd Boulevard was a dirt road, and mail was delivered twice a day to an RFD box located on Augusta Road. Traveling gypsies would camp on the rocky area behind the home and would come by the house for water. (Courtesy of Elizabeth Peace Stall.)

SNOW DAY. Betty Peace looks at her brother Bony carrying a pellet gun while playing in the snow. On snow days, the large hill on Byrd Boulevard would be blocked off to allow for safe, uninterrupted sledding. (Courtesy of Elizabeth Peace Stall.)

ANDERSON RESIDENCE. Built for Mr. and Mrs. Waddy Anderson, this home with its large pond in the front was designed by Joseph Gilbert Cunningham. Among the many commercial and residential buildings he designed during his career were the Imperial Hotel on Washington Street and the Finlay Building on Main Street. Among Cunningham's most noted projects were the Greenville Memorial Auditorium and the Trinity Lutheran Church. After his brother's death, Joseph practiced alone until his retirement in 1956. He passed away in 1964. (Courtesy of the author.)

CLUB DRIVE. Sandra Stansell stands alongside her younger brother Danny in the front yard of their home on Club Drive. The Stansell home has remained in the family since it was built in 1942. (Courtesy of Laney Stansell.)

DOUBLE WEDDING. Brothers and sisters play dress-up in the Meyers Park neighborhood. Pictured, from left to right, are David Hudson, Mary Ann Lee, Buist Hudson, and Jim Lee. (Courtesy of Patricia W. Howard.)

MEYERS DRIVE. Neighbors gather to play in the snow. Pictured, from left to right, are Patricia Williams, David Hudson, Ida Hudson, George Rigby, Margaret Williams, Midge Williams, and Nancy Williams. (Courtesy of Patricia W. Howard.)

MARSHALL FOREST GARDEN CLUB. Organized in 1951 by the ladies of the neighborhood, the Marshall Forest Garden Club held educational meetings, holiday socials, and community service efforts, including beautifying Blythe Elementary School, planting 6,700 bulbs in the neighborhood, and grounds-keeping of the neighborhood parkway. (Courtesy of the Marshall Forest Garden Club.)

CLUB PROGRAM. The Marshall Forest Garden Club would hold annual shows and contests throughout the year at a neighbor's home. Members would be given specific tasks with a set of guidelines they must abide by, and their peers would judge them using a point system. One such contest was arranging certain varieties of flowers in a Coca-Cola bottle. (Courtesy of the Marshall Forest Garden Club.)

AUTUMN HOUSE

THE ANNUAL FLOWER SHOW

of the

MARSHALL FOREST GARDEN CLUB

at the

home of

MRS. JULIAN HUNT

349 Riverside Drive

4:00 P. M. to 5:30 P. M.

Wednesday, October 9, 1963

Mrs. N. A. Price, Jr., Chairman

Mrs. Fred Land, Co-Chairman

STREET SIGNS. As reported in the August 1, 1957, edition of the *Piedmont Paper*, nine of the ten newly erected street signs in Marshall Forest had been vandalized and stolen. The article mentions that the garden club asked "Greenville people to look around and see if they can locate the missing signs." (Courtesy of the Marshall Forest Garden Club.)

KIWANIS PARK. Located next to Blythe Elementary on the corner of Augusta and Old Augusta Roads, Kiwanis Park has been open to the public for recreation for over 60 years. Seen here, Lottie Brown and Vanda Outlaw prepare lunches for the youth of Augusta Heights Baptist Church. (Courtesy of Augusta Heights Baptist Church.)

CRYSTAL AVENUE. The Reverend and Mrs. Archibald Clinch Odom house was the first home built on Crystal Avenue in 1938. Seen here from left to right are three generations of the Odom family—A.C., Edgar, and newborn Robert. (Courtesy of the author.)

ODOM RESIDENCE. Located at the corner of Old Augusta Road and Crystal Avenue, the home of Edgar and Mildred Odom was the second house built on Crystal Avenue in the Pleasant Valley neighborhood. Pleasant Valley was developed by builder Easton Rogers. (Courtesy of the author.)

PLEASANT VALLEY NEIGHBORHOOD CHILDREN. Pictured here in the 1940s, children gather to play in the Pleasant Valley neighborhood. From left to right are (first row) Patsy Childers, Dwight Odom, Judy Clark, and Jerry Skelton; (second row) Peralee Elkins, Judy Heatwoll, Robert Odom, and Raye Clark; (third row) Barbara Jo Elkins. (Courtesy of the author.)

WHITE CHRISTMAS. Children celebrate the snow during Christmas. From left to right are Dwight Odom, Peralee Elkins, Robert Odom, Raye Clark, and Judy Clark. (Courtesy of the author.)

PAPERBOY. On his Schwinn bicycle, nine-year-old Dwight Odom delivered the *Piedmont Paper* six days a week to 86 homes in Traxler Park. (Courtesy of the author.)

ENTRANCE AT CHANTICLEER. The main entrance off of Faris Road consists of lush landscaping and two semicircular brick walls adorned by concrete Chanticleer roosters on either side of Michaux Drive. The name *Chanitcleer* was taken from Geoffrey Chaucer's *Canterbury Tales'* "Nun's Priest's Tale" about a rooster and a fox. The rooster's name in the story is Chanticleer, which means "clear singing" in French. A not-so-time-honored tradition of the area is the removal of the roosters from the entrance. To combat this perpetual problem, the developer would keep a surplus of these concrete birds on hand. A sales office was constructed by the developer at the entrance but was removed in 1968. (Courtesy of the author.)

WILLIAM COXE AERIAL. Prior to the development of Chanticleer and the Greenville Hospital system, this land was once part of the Frank Earle family farm. The Earle property was primarily used for growing cotton and raising livestock. During the development of Chanticleer, evidence of the farm was unearthed, and the terraced fields can still be seen along Chapman Road. The untouched acreage was prime hunting land for some, and children from nearby Pleasant Valley found it ideal for overnight camping and exploration. Others used the land for more sinister activities, such as distilling moonshine. (Courtesy of Hughes Development.)

CHANTICLEER, SECTIONS ONE THROUGH SEVEN. In the early 1960s, brothers Jack and Robert "Red" Hughes purchased the property from Frank Earle's widow, Grace. Much thought was put into the development of Chanticleer, with the roads designed to preserve the natural beauty of the area. Michaux Drive is laid out in a curvilinear fashion in order to create a leisurely drive into the neighborhood. Many of the streets were named after botanists and naturalists, including Bartram, Catesby, and LeConte. (Courtesy of Hughes Development.)

McCOY HOUSE. The McCoy House is the second home to be built on Lowood Lane along the eighth fairway. The original owner attended Queens College, situated in the historic Myers Park area of Charlotte, North Carolina. The owner asked architect Earle Gauldin to replicate a home close to that campus when designing this house. (Courtesy of Hughes Development.)

SULLIVAN RESIDENCE. The owners of the Sullivan residence, situated on the 17th green on DeBrahm Court, were given the second opportunity to purchase any lot along the golf course. Like Eagle Avenue off of Crescent Avenue, this street name has been misspelled in county records, resulting in the misspelled name becoming the official name of the street. (Courtesy of Hughes Development.)

TORNADO. On a spring afternoon in March 1978, a large tornado touched down resulting in the major destruction of a number of homes in Chanticleer. Some residents had to move temporarily while their homes were being rebuilt. (Courtesy of Hughes Development.)

Four

SCHOOLS AND CHURCHES

AUGUSTA ROAD BAPTIST CHURCH. During Augusta Road's first development boom in the 1920s, members from two Baptist churches, Greenville First and Pendleton Street, came together to form a new Baptist church in the area. In April 1924, a meeting was held at the home of Mrs. C.E. Hatch on McDaniel Avenue. In attendance were Mrs. Hatch, Mrs. E.N. Whitmire, Furman Norris, A.G. Furman, and Mrs. J.T. Woodson, among others. A committee comprised of members from both parent churches was appointed to acquire property at the intersection of Augusta Road and Jones Avenue. (Courtesy of the Greenville County Historical Society, Coxe Collection.)

AUGUSTA ROAD BAPTIST CHURCH, GREENVILLE, S. C.

BIRTHPLACE, 1924

OUR PRESENT HOME

WFBC
S. S. Lesson Program
Saturdays
8:00 - 8:30 A. M.

"The Victorious Life Church"

"To the Praise of the Glory of His Grace"

OUR GOAL, 1944 (D.V.)

Annual Bible Conference
Mar. 29-Apr. 5, 1935

Speakers

Wm. R. Newell,
DeLand

Ernest N. Wadsworth
Chicago

Isaac Page
China

ARBC POSTCARD. For the first several months after organization, Augusta Road Baptist held its services in a church-owned bungalow on Jones Avenue, which later became the parsonage. A new, three-story educational building was constructed on the property at Jones Avenue and Augusta Road in August 1925. In 1949, the sanctuary was added to the front of the educational building, facing the corner of the intersection. It was designed differently from the goal of 1944. (Courtesy of Augusta Road Baptist Church.)

BIBLE PRESBYTERIAN CHURCH. This church was built in 1941, and it was difficult to source iron to construct the rafters during World War II rationing, nearly causing the construction to be canceled. The two-story, clapboard building attached to the rear was replaced by the Gothic-style, arched, brick breezeway seen today. The church has also been the sanctuary for Augusta Street Presbyterian Church and currently, Paramount Park Baptist Church. (Courtesy of the Greenville County Historical Society, Coxe Collection.)

GREENVILLE SENIOR HIGH SCHOOL. Through a federal grant of $420,000 courtesy of the Works Progress Administration, a new Greenville High School was built. The three-story, yellow brick building was designed by the J.E. Sirrine Company with a center courtyard. Completed on August 28, 1938, the modern high school welcomed 1,300 students in 9th through 11th grades. The school was referred to as the senior high school, as the Westfield Street School had become the junior high school. Twelfth grade was first offered during the 1947–1948 school year, and ninth grade was then moved to Westfield Street. Students in the class of 1947 were offered the option of graduating or continuing on to the 12th grade. The school was integrated in 1970. (Both, courtesy of the Greenville County Historical Society, Coxe and Landing Collections.)

GHS Auditorium. The Greenville High School Auditorium has been a venue for many plays and musicals for over 80 years. These productions in particular were directed by Dr. DuPre Rhame. Upon receiving a bachelor of music degree from Furman University, he went on to study at the Eastman School of Music and Julliard. He returned to Greenville in 1925 to teach at Furman University and did so until his retirement in 1970. Along with teaching at Furman University, DuPre directed school plays and the chorus at Greenville High School. (Both, courtesy of the Greenville County Historical Society, Coxe Collection.)

GREENVILLE HIGH ART CLASS. This art class copies a sculpture in the center of the photograph. The classroom is complete with a human skeleton. (Courtesy of the Greenville County Historical Society, Coxe Collection.)

HOME ECONOMICS CLASS. Three Greenville High School students demonstrate the steps in making a skirt in home economics class. Classmate Lucile Smith begins cutting out the garment, while Barbara Hannon sews, and Enid Smith presses. (Courtesy of Greenville High School.)

NAUTILUS TREE. A Greenville High landmark, the Nautilus tree still stands today and is a common backdrop for superlatives and club photographs used in the *Nautilus* yearbook. (Courtesy of Greenville High School.)

SIRRINE STADIUM GROUND-BREAKING CEREMONY. Spectators and a marching band stand in the vacant lot and listen to city leaders describe the new Sirrine Stadium at the ground-breaking ceremony. In the background, homes along Cleveland Street and Jones Avenue can be seen, while only a curb cut exists where Ben Street is today. (Courtesy of the Greenville County Historical Society, Coxe Collection.)

SIRRINE STADIUM. Located at the corner of University Ridge and Cleveland Street, Sirrine Stadium was a joint project between the City of Greenville and Furman University, with funding made possible by the Works Progress Administration. Furman University alumnus J.E. Sirrine spearheaded fundraising with fellow alumni. Morris–McCoy Construction Company began building the stadium in 1935, and the first game was played on Halloween 1936, with Furman University defeating Davidson College. The official dedication of the stadium was on November 14, 1936, with Furman University beating the University of South Carolina. After all construction bonds were retired in 1946, the stadium came into full possession of Furman University. When the school moved to its new campus in 1958, it ceased to play games there—only Greenville High School used the stadium. In 1981, Sam Francis led a campaign to raise $650,000 to purchase the property from Furman University and transfer the ownership to the Greenville County School District. (Both, courtesy of the Greenville County Historical Society, Coxe Collection.)

DONALDSON SCHOOL. Built in 1917 as an elementary school on Tindal Avenue, the Donaldson School was built on land donated by Jacob Cagle to complement his Cagle Park neighborhood. Construction was delayed for one year due to a lawsuit over the location of the school, which was claimed to be too far out in the country. The school was named for Thomas Quinton Donaldson, who served as the first chair of the Greenville County School Board in 1886. In 1939, Albert Einstein was asked to speak to the student body upon the request of Furman University scientist John R. Sampey, whose daughter was in the fifth grade. Einstein was in Greenville visiting his son H. Albert, who was living and working in Greenville at the time. Einstein's advice to the students was to learn "only what they could not find in books." (Both, courtesy of the Greenville County Historical Society, Coxe and Landing Collections.)

ST. MICHAEL LUTHERAN CHURCH. On February 15, 1948, a small group of members from Trinity Lutheran set out to build a new church on Augusta Street. With 65 people present, the first service was held on April 25 in the basement of the home of Mr. and Mrs. William M. Schwartz at 104 West Augusta Place. The church was formally organized and named on June 27, and services were moved to the Furman University chapel that August. That same month, the church purchased three lots along Augusta Street in the Traxler Park neighborhood at a total cost of $6,000. In January 1949, Philadelphia architect T. Norman Mansell was hired to make preliminary drawings of the church, and H.L. McLendon was hired to complete the construction drawings. The first service was held on Palm Sunday, April 2, 1950, with the pews and carpeting being installed right up to time of the service. In 1971, architects Craig, Gauldin, and Davis, along with contractor M.L. Garrett, were hired to design and construct the sanctuary seen today. (Courtesy of the Greenville County Historical Society, Elrod Collection.)

AUGUSTA CIRCLE SCHOOL. In August 1922, Augusta Road residents did not live in the city and had to pay tuition to attend Donaldson School. Residents petitioned the city's school board to open a new school within the area, and the motion was approved. Melville Westervelt was developing the Augusta Circle neighborhood on the former John Davenport 32-acre farm and donated a lot on Winyah Street at Tomassee for the school—and to help boost sales. The school board approved the site in January 1923. The architectural firm Beacham and LeGrand was selected to design the school, and Gallivan Construction Company was selected to build it. The original two-story building was constructed of dark brick and limestone edging and housed four classrooms. (Courtesy of the Greenville County Historical Society Coxe Collection.)

1939 VOLLEYBALL CHAMPIONS. The girls' volleyball team poses for a photograph at the front door of Augusta Circle School in 1939. Although the school was named Augusta Circle, the building was dedicated to Otis Prentiss Mills. His name and the date of the school are inscribed above the front door. (Courtesy of Augusta Circle School.)

CIRCLE NEWS. The sixth-grade class of 1941 edits the *Circle News*. The Augusta Circle School originally opened with grades first through third. Fourth grade attended Donaldson School. (Courtesy of Augusta Circle School.)

ARBOR DAY. Fourth graders and adults gather to plant an oak tree outside Augusta Circle in 1942. Included in the group are Jim Aull, Hugh Croxton, Ethel Mae Smeak, Betty Peace, and Joyce Hiller. In 1924, the Augusta Road Community Club was formed by ladies in the area in support of the school. (Courtesy of Betty Peace Stall.)

AUGUSTA CIRCLE PARADE FLOAT. Throughout the 1950s, Augusta Circle entered a float in the Greenville Christmas parade along Main Street. Several of the school's prize-winning floats were constructed with the help of servicemen stationed at Donaldson Air Force Base. (Courtesy of Augusta Circle School.)

AUGUSTA CIRCLE PAPER DRIVE. In the mid-1950s, the Parent-Teacher Association (PTA) petitioned city council to provide crossing guards at busy traffic sections near the school. The request was denied, but parents and teachers continued to persevere. The PTA began to hold paper drives to fund the salary for off-duty policemen to protect the students. Their creative problem-solving gained them accolades in the *Piedmont Paper*. Pictured sorting paper from left to right are Ronnie Stovall, Mike Howell, and Mrs. Heyward Morgan. (Courtesy of Augusta Circle School.)

TRINITY UNITED METHODIST CHURCH. The Trinity United Methodist Church was a result of the development boom along Augusta Road after World War II. On August 25, 1947, a group of citizens wanting to establish a Methodist church met at Augusta Circle School. The newly formed congregation adopted the name Memorial Methodist, in honor of those who lost their lives in the war. In February 1948, the 95-member congregation began construction of a one-story, flat-roofed, concrete structure at the corner of Country Club Drive and Augusta Road while at the same time conducting regular services at Augusta Circle School. The first service was held in the new building on September 19, 1948, and the name of the church was officially changed to Trinity United Methodist. (Courtesy of Trinity United Methodist Church.)

TRINITY UNITED METHODIST PARSONAGE. In the fall of 1948, the congregation had a parsonage constructed on West Faris Road for its first pastor, David Reese Jr. The next two decades that followed saw rapid growth, and in the early 1960s, the parsonage itself was moved to Augusta Street. (Courtesy of Trinity United Methodist Church.)

TRINITY METHODIST SANCTUARY. Members of the congregation stand in front of the altar of the sanctuary, which was completed in October 1955 at a cost of $123,000 fully furnished. Rev. R.C. Griffith stands behind the podium. Griffith served as pastor from September 1957 to June 1961. (Courtesy of Trinity United Methodist Church.)

TRINITY SERVICE. The congregation sings a hymn along with the choir in the church sanctuary. Two years after the completion of the first building, plans were drawn for a second floor with a brick veneer and pitched roof. Architectural firm Cunningham and Walker drew all phases including the present sanctuary, social hall, and church offices. The first service in the new building was held on October 23, 1955. (Courtesy of Trinity United Methodist Church.)

BLYTHE ELEMENTARY SIXTH-GRADE CLASS. As a result of overcrowding at Augusta Circle School, the Greenville School Board decided to purchase 18 acres of the R.I. Woodside property located on the west side of Augusta Road. Completed in 1951, the building was designed by the architectural firm of Lineburger and Ferrester and had a capacity of 385 students. The school was named for Edgeworth Montague Blythe, who taught school in Greenville from 1891 to 1893 and later served on the Greenville County School System Board of Trustees for 14 years. (Courtesy of Blythe Academy of Languages.)

BLYTHE ELEMENTARY CROSSING GUARDS. With the school built with only one entrance located on Long Hill Street, students walking or riding to school from the east side of Augusta had to travel an extra five to six blocks to get to the school. As the lack of a road was becoming a hazard, the school board requested that the city construct an access road from Augusta Road, which was granted and completed in 1953. (Courtesy of Blythe Academy of Languages.)

OPERATION DEEP FREEZE. A new, school-wide volunteer project involving students and airmen came into being with Operation Deep Freeze. Children on the Donaldson Air Force Base who attended Blythe Elemenary gathered Christmas presents for Donaldson's C-124 crew to deliver to families living in the Arctic. With temperatures 20 degrees below zero, pilots would have to land supply planes on ice strips. (Both, courtesy of Blythe Academy of Languages.)

Augusta Heights Baptist Ground-Breaking. After World War II, the Greenville County Baptist Association saw the need for a new church in the growing southern end of Augusta Road. Furman University president Dr. John L. Plyler instructed Rev. J.T. Gillespie to hold a meeting to seek interest in the church. In attendance were community residents as well as ministers from Augusta Road, Earle Street, Pendleton Street, and First Baptist Churches. On October 3, 1950, the name Augusta Heights was adopted, and regular meetings were held at Payne Brothers' Dairy, while Sunday school classes and worship services were held at Augusta Circle School. A building committee was formed on October 15, 1950, and a dedication was held on April 9, 1951, on the 3.5-acre site purchased from Augusta Road Baptist with a $10,000 gift from First Baptist Church. (Courtesy of Augusta Heights Baptist Church.)

Laying Cornerstone. On April 13, 1952, the cornerstone was laid following the Easter service. Two marble slabs were placed—one bearing the name of the board of deacons, and the other inscribed with the name of the church, the date erected, and the name of the pastor. A time capsule was deposited in the cornerstone containing the list of charter members, a history of the church, newspaper clippings regarding the church, and special bulletins. Shown laying the cornerstone are builder Fred Carr (left), building committee chair Fletcher Stone, and pastor L. Edward Smith. (Courtesy of Augusta Heights Baptist Church.)

MRS. STREET'S SUNDAY SCHOOL CLASS. In the late 1950s, Augusta Heights Sunday school classes were overflowing into the homes of nearby residents and across the street to Payne's Dairy. Pictured here is Mrs. Street's Sunday school class. Construction of an educational building was completed on February 5, 1961. It was the first building in Greenville to be constructed with prestressed concrete beams in lieu of conventional steel beams. (Courtesy of Augusta Heights Baptist Church.)

AUGUSTA HEIGHTS SANCTUARY. On May 5, 1963, ground was broken for a new sanctuary. Charles Potter was hired to design the building, and Chester Reece was hired to construct it. With seating for over 1,000, the new sanctuary was dedicated on July 12, 1964. (Courtesy of Augusta Heights Baptist Church.)

HUGHES JUNIOR HIGH. Due to overcrowding at Westfield Street Junior High, the school board voted to build a junior high in the growing Augusta Road area. The school was built on land donated by the Iselin family that was once part of the McBee farm called Brushy Creek. The school opened in 1956 and was named for Charles E. Hughes, who had been a teacher and principal in the Greenville County School System. (Both, courtesy of Hughes Academy.)

WESTMINSTER PRESBYTERIAN TENT. In May 1947, 23 members of First Presbyterian Greenville met to form a new church in the growing Augusta Road area. Among the members of the group, Dan W. Cochrane offered a parcel of land fronting Augusta Road. The group decided that once 100 individuals signed up for membership, it would apply for organization through the Enoree Presbytery. By July, the church had 101 members, and in August, a tent was pitched on the southeast corner of the property, where the Enoree Presbytery met to form the new church. The tent would continue to be used for worship, with services be held in the evening during summer months. Snakes and neighborhood dogs would enter the tent, and the occasional lightning storm would pop the lights. (Courtesy of Westminster Presbyterian Church.)

THE BASEMENT. The Basement was named due to the thought that as funds became available, an upper floor would be added. With the first service held on December 14, 1947, the simple structure, built of concrete block and brick, held a bathroom, kitchen, nine classrooms, and a large room for worship. (Courtesy of Westminster Presbyterian Church.)

WESTMINSTER PRESBYTERIAN CHURCH. Soon, the congregation began to outgrow the confines of the Basement. A building committee was formed, and shortly thereafter, the architectural firm Logan and Williams was hired to design the first permanent structure. The building committee chose the architectural style of modified Gothic, which allows for a modern interpretation while preserving a sense of tradition. During construction, worship was held at Augusta Circle School and the Plaza Theatre, which was said to be so dark that only familiar hymns were sung. The first service in the new building was held on Easter Sunday, April 9, 1950. (Courtesy of Westminster Presbyterian Church.)

COCHRANE HOUSE. By February 1952, the church was over capacity, and another building committee was formed to determine immediate and long-term needs. It was decided that the remainder of the Cochrane property, located at the corner of Augusta Street and West Augusta Place, with 348 feet along Augusta Street, would be needed in order to accomplish future goals. After the death of Minnie Phipps Cochrane in January 1958, the church came into possession of the home and used it for immediate needs for classroom space. (Courtesy of Westminster Presbyterian Church.)

OLD AND NEW CHURCH. On March 30, 1959, church architect Harold E. Wagoner of Philadelphia was hired to create a master plan, with the local firm Beachman and Wood to prepare the drawings, while Yeargin Construction Company was hired for building. The capital campaign to fund the project was headed by Greenville business leader and philanthropist Arthur Magill. (Courtesy of Westminster Presbyterian Church.)

BUILDING COMMITTEE. A ground-breaking ceremony was held on November 19, 1961. Seen here are, from left to right, John Haley (pastor), Betty Richbourg, Tom Biggs (assistant pastor), Martha Carpenter, John Marshall, Eugene Beach (associate to Wagoner), Robert Yeargin, Arthur Magill, and Harold Wagoner. (Courtesy of Westminster Presbyterian Church.)

ARCHES AND STEEPLE. As the tall, arched beams were being erected, people joked that Westminster was building a gigantic McDonald's. (Courtesy of Westminster Presbyterian Church.)

WESTMINSTER'S NEW SANCTUARY. The dedication of the Westminster sanctuary was held on March 24, 1963. The stained-glass windows were designed by pastor John Haley and crafted by Willet Studios of Philadelphia. The brightly colored pieces of glass range in size and thickness and are chipped and faceted to control light. The bell tower stands 151 feet high to the cross on top. The carillon and tower were donated by Malcolm P. Niven. (Courtesy of Westminster Presbyterian Church.)

Five

GRAND ESTATES

WILKINS HOUSE. This house was built in 1868 by renowned Greenville contractor Jacob Cagle for William and Harriett Cleveland Wilkins. The home fronting Augusta Street was designed in the Second Empire style, a popular Victorian style borrowed from the French during the reign of Napoleon III. An attached conservatory housed coleus plants that were brought out each spring and placed in rows of white and pink on each side of the front steps. A barn on the property housed two black horses and three cows, while peacocks strutted on the front lawn. (Courtesy of the Greenville County Historical Society, Coxe Collection.)

WILKINS HOME INTERIOR. The interior of the home featured ornate, gas-lit chandeliers, velvet draperies surrounding the doorways and windows, and heavy, arched cornices and large intricate moldings. There were four grand rooms on the main floor that were decorated with embossed wallpaper, Victorian furniture, paintings, and ferns and other tropical plants from the conservatory. A carved, curving staircase led to the family's private quarters on the second floor. (Courtesy of the Greenville County Historical Society, Landing Collection.)

WILKINS HOME. William Wilkins was a prosperous businessman involved in several Greenville ventures including, but not limited to, Wilkins, Poe, and Company Hardware; *Greenville Daily News*; and the ill-fated Opera House, located at the corner of Main Street and McBee Avenue, that burned only a few months after completion. William died in 1895, and Harriett lived another 35 years in the home until her death in 1930. In 1933, the Wilkins home was leased by the family to R.D. Jones, who both resided in the home and used the main floor for his funeral business until the 1990s. (Courtesy of the Greenville County Library, South Carolina Room.)

O.P. MILLS HOUSE. The home of Otis Prentiss and Susan Cordelia Gower Mills was designed in the Queen Anne style of Victorian architecture and was situated on 300 acres that make up Otis, Prentiss, and Mills Avenues. Mills was an entrepreneur, owning nearby South Carolina Cottonseed Oil Company, Mills Mill, and Millsdale Dairy. The dairy, which raised Guernsey cows, sold milk, cream, and butter throughout Greenville County. A believer in education, Prentiss built two mills and a YMCA in his mill village. Due to his philanthropy in the community, the school board honored him posthumously by naming the Augusta Circle School building after him. (Courtesy of the Greenville County Historical Society, Coxe Collection.)

IVY LAWN. The Williams–Earle house, known as Ivy Lawn or Holly Hill, originally sat on 43 acres located on modern-day Grove Road and situated along Brushy Creek. Construction began in 1820, and the current two-story, T-shaped building was completed in 1850. The Greek Revival home was originally constructed by Dr. Thomas Williams, a prominent Greenville physician and landowner who also served in the state legislature. Richard Harrison Earle, grandson of Col. Elias Earle, purchased the property in 1880. The property was listed in the National Register of Historic Places on July 1, 1982. (Courtesy of Thomas Riddle.)

WILLIAMS–EARLE SLAVE CABIN. Built in the 1840s, the two-room cabin was originally used for slaves on the property but later served as a home for African American freedmen from the time of emancipation until the 1930s. In 2009, the cabin was moved to the Roper Mountain Science Center and rehabilitated through a joint effort between the History Channel, the National Trust for Historic Preservation, the Greenville County Historic Preservation Commission, and the Greenville County School System. (Courtesy of Thomas Riddle.)

LANNEAU–NORWOOD HOUSE. Born in Charleston, Charles H. Lanneau came to Greenville in the late 1800s to serve as treasurer of the Reedy River Factory. Lanneau purchased 56 acres of land in 1872, and in 1876, he built this three-story, brick, Second Empire–style home. Lanneau furthered his lucrative textile career through other ventures, including the Huguenot Mill, and served as secretary of Vardy Cotton Mills. He also started a mill and small village not far from his home on what is now Lanneau Drive and Camille Avenue. (Courtesy of the Greenville County Library, South Carolina Room.)

LANNEAU–NORWOOD OUTBUILDING. Lanneau sold the home in 1907 to local banker John Wilkins Norwood. Norwood started the Greenville Trust and Savings Company in 1906, and later became the vice president of American Spinning. Mrs. Norwood was against the purchase of the property, citing that it was too far from town. The Norwoods added a kitchen inside the home, along with electricity and telephone. The home remains in the Norwood family to this day. (Courtesy of the Greenville County Library, South Carolina Room.)

ALTA VISTA. In 1926, John Norwood began to develop his surrounding property into the Alta Vista neighborhood. Vacant lots and streets freshly paved in concrete can be seen, while the land surrounding Cleveland Street is rural farmland. The Wilkins–Norwood home is visible on the left. (Courtesy of the Greenville County Historical Society, Coxe Collection.)

MCKISSICK HOUSE. This house was built by Atlanta architect Philip Trammell Schutze in 1939 for Ellison and Jean McKissick. Schutze received degrees in architecture from both Georgia Tech and Columbia University and did postgraduate training in classical studies at the American Academy in Rome, Italy. He also designed the Charles E. Daniel home, White Oaks, which now serves as the president's home at Furman University and the Swan House in Atlanta, which is owned by the Atlanta Historical Society. Jean owned the house until her death in 1991, at which time ownership was transferred to Christ Episcopal Church. (Courtesy of the Greenville County Historical Society, Coxe Collection.)

BALENTINE MANSION. Built in 1938 for William Louis and Annie Lou Gibson Balentine, the Williamsburg-style home was constructed by Annie's father, Joe D. Gibson, and designed by Tog Smith, who worked for the Department of the Interior and helped design the Natchez Trace Parkway. On 4.5 acres of what was once part of the former Addams Plantation, the home has hosted three family weddings and remains in the family to this day. (Courtesy of the Martin –Huffman family.)

WYCHE MANSION. Built in 1931 for Greenville attorney C. Granville Wyche, this house was designed by Atlanta architect Silas D. Trowbridge. Built as a country estate for his large family, the Wyche Mansion is an example of Depression-era Italian Renaissance architecture. It also boasts a Beaux-Arts influence through its large portico, balustrades, and grouped Classical -style columns. The home was built with a small grotto and pool that was bordered by large boulders and cement mortar inscribed with the names of Wyche's children. Trowbridge also designed an elaborate formal garden, but it was never carried out by the Wyches. Mrs. Wyche lived in the home until 1988. It was listed in the National Register of Historic Places on September 2, 1993. (Courtesy of the author.)

BRUSHY CREEK. Brushy Creek was built in 1836 by Vardry McBee on an 11,020-acre tract of land he purchased from Lemuel Alston. The 1.5-story, frame farmhouse is typical of those built in the upstate during the 19th century. The original portion of the home consists of four downstairs rooms, a wide central hall, and two rooms upstairs. The original kitchen was constructed separately at the rear of the home and was joined to the house in 1924 by a single room. The property also included a gristmill, complete with waterwheel, brick potting shed, log barn, and a well house. Vardry McBee is considered Greenville's founding father, who donated land for the Baptist, Methodist, Episcopal, and Presbyterian churches in downtown. In 1872, his son Alexander purchased the property, which then consisted of 672 acres. Along with being a banker and businessman, Alexander served as mayor of Greenville and in the state legislature. The home remained in the McBee family until 1923, when the house and 120 acres were sold to textile manufacturer Robert I. Woodside, but it was sold back to Alexander's daughter Sarah McBee Beck in 1932. (Courtesy of Judy Iselin Cromwell.)

ISELIN FAMILY. Seated on the running board are, from left to right, Fannie H., Judy, William Jay, and John Jay Iselin with family dog Lady. In 1938, the Becks sold the home along with 44.75 acres to William Jay Iselin. Iselin was associated with Woodside Mills and tragically died in a private plane crash outside Washington, DC, in 1951. The home remains in the Iselin family today and was placed in the National Register of Historic Places in 1999. (Courtesy of Judy Iselin Cromwell.)

GRISTMILL. Complete with waterwheel, a fully operational gristmill was located on Brushy Creek. The land beyond the mill was later donated by Mrs. Iselin for the building of Hughes Middle School. (Courtesy of Judy Iselin Cromwell.)

PICNIC BY THE MILL. A group of family and friends joins together for a picnic by the gristmill. The mill was later razed, and the creek was dammed in order to create a pond. During the winter months, the Iselins would allow families from Donaldson Air Force Base to ice-skate on the pond, and neighborhood children would wade in the pool during summer months. (Courtesy of Judy Iselin Cromwell.)

GUARDING THE CAR. Two goats stand on the hood of the family vehicle as if they are watching over it. Many types of livestock were raised on the farm, including chickens, mules, and pigs. (Courtesy of Judy Iselin Cromwell.)

Buggy Ride. John Jay and younger sister Judy ride in a carriage pulled by Tony, the family mule. In the mid-1960s, Judy and her husband, David Cromwell, purchased the home from her mother and took on a renovation of the house and grounds, adding elaborate walls and walks constructed of brick reclaimed from the Camperdown Cotton Mill. John Jay grew up to become a pioneer in public television. Among his many accomplishments, Queen Elizabeth II awarded him an honorary Commander of the Order of the British Empire in recognition of his outstanding contribution to British television interests in the United States. (Courtesy of Judy Iselin Cromwell.)

Six

A Tale of Two Golf Courses

Teeing Off. Greenville Country Club head-professional Dave Ferguson tees a ball on a sand tee box on what is now the 14th fairway at Riverside. The club's roots date back to 1895, when a group of eight to ten men headed up to Piney Mountain to clear a nine-hole golf course on approximately 50 acres of land they had acquired from an Indian tribe. Maintenance and upkeep of the course included a herd of sheep. This group of men, including Will Sirrine, Perry Beattie, and Edge Blythe, came to be known as the "Piney Mountain Pioneers." By 1904, as many as 50 golfers were frequenting the course. (Courtesy of the Greenville County Historical Society, Coxe Collection.)

PUTTING. By 1905, the group at Piney Mountain felt it was time to pursue a more modern facility fit for recreation and social events. The group, led by later club president Capt. Ellison Adger Smyth, formed a stock company to lease and later purchase the 57-acre estate and mansion of former governor Benjamin Perry called Sans Souci, built in 1871. (Courtesy of the Greenville County Historical Society, Coxe Collection.)

RELAXING AFTER A ROUND. The Victorian mansion was reconfigured to become an exquisite clubhouse, including dining facilities, a bar, a large hall for parties, locker rooms, and even sleeping quarters for overnight stays. A nine-hole course was built and redesigned in 1915 by J.E. Sirrine to eliminate crossing fairways. (Courtesy of the Greenville Country Club.)

NEW HOME. As other clubs began to open around the state in the late 1910s, members of Sans Souci began to want comparable facilities. Around the same time, Greenville developer David Byrd Traxler approached the club with an offer of 158 acres within his new development, Traxler Park. Traxler offered the tract of land for $10, with the requirement that the members would build and operate a country club and golf course for a period of 13 years, after which the club would own the land free and clear. (Courtesy of the Greenville County Historical Society, Coxe Collection.)

THE NEW CLUBHOUSE AND FACILITIES. The new clubhouse and facilities, which included tennis courts, swimming pool, and an 18-hole golf course, opened in 1923. The name was officially changed to Greenville Country Club (GCC) in 1927. In this 1949 photograph, the golf superintendent's house can be seen to the right of the parking lot; and the future home of Wilton McKinney, one of the club's tennis professionals, is located across Byrd Boulevard from the clubhouse. Tennis professional Wilton McKinney is located across Byrd Boulevard from the clubhouse. The then No. 18 green is situated below the tennis courts. (Courtesy of the Greenville Country Club.)

ALONG THE REEDY. In 1830, D. Townsend Smith's Woodlands Plantation grew and sold more than 16,000 pounds of rice grown on his 25 acres of marshland along the Reedy River. The plantation's cow chutes, barns, and pigsties were located at present-day Byrd Boulevard. (Courtesy of the Greenville County Historical Society, Coxe Collection.)

FAMILY SWIMMING. The club's first pool was located at the site of the modern-day lower parking lot. The pool was drained each week on Sunday night and refilled on Tuesday from water pumped in from Rock Creek. It is said that the pool's first lifeguard did not know how to swim. (Courtesy of the Greenville Country Club.)

CAPTAIN JOE. Joseph E. Sirrine, or "Captain Joe," congratulates winner Lewis Johnson and runner-up Frank Ford at the 1937 Carolinas Amateur Golf Tournament held at the Greenville Country Club. Known as the "father to Greenville Country Club," Sirrine was the third club president, serving for 30 years from 1912 to 1942. To keep the club open during the years of the Great Depression, Joseph personally paid its expenses. (Courtesy of the Greenville County Historical Society, Coxe Collection.)

CLUBHOUSE TERRACE. The terrace was a place to gather and unwind. Seen here are two women golfers celebrating after a tournament. (Courtesy of the Greenville County Historical Society.)

PAUL G. CUSHMAN. An avid golfer, Paul G. Cushman won the club championship in 1934. He was president of the South Carolina Golf Association and an advocate for the game throughout the state. (Courtesy of the Greenville Country Club.)

JANE COTHRAN. Considered the first great golfer to come out of the Upstate, Jane was the niece of Joseph E. Sirrine. Cothran grew up playing the game. She was the no. 1 golfer for Greenville High School and won the ladies' club championship while she was a senior. Her achievements include winning three Biltmore Country Club Invitational's from 1931 to 1939, setting the women's course record in 1940 shooting a men's par of 70, and placing second in the 1940 Women's National played at Pebble Beach. (Courtesy of the Greenville Country Club.)

NUMBER ONE. A group of spectators watches Walter Chandler tee off during the 1949 Club Championship. An unpaved Byrd Boulevard can be seen running parallel to the fairway that is now No. 12. (Courtesy of the Greenville Country Club.)

AWARDS CEREMONY. A young Billy Delk receives his trophy after a tournament. Delk later became head professional at Pebble Creek Country Club. (Courtesy of the Greenville Country Club.)

CLUBHOUSE. In 1939, the clubhouse was refurbished. The covered porch on the rear of the building was enclosed for year-round dining. Black tie with white dinner jackets was the standard dress for the waitstaff. The large hall could serve a variety of purposes including dining, meetings, and parties. In 1954, this clubhouse would be replaced with the one seen today. (Both, courtesy of the Greenville Country Club.)

ANNUAL MEETING. Members gather for a buffet-style dinner before the club's annual meeting. (Courtesy of the Greenville Country Club.)

SUMMER DINING. During warmer months, meals would be served on the clubhouse terrace. Members dressed in summer-weight suits, and ladies wore large hats. (Courtesy of the Greenville Country Club.)

TROPHY. Laura Echols Dupont, surrounded by friends and colleagues, accepts a trophy. (Courtesy of the Greenville Country Club.)

GALLERY. Spectators in the gallery watch a doubles tennis match on the hill below the clubhouse. (Courtesy of the Greenville Country Club.)

TENNIS MATCH. Judges officiate a tennis match at court one. The club originally started with four clay courts at its Traxler Park site, which has now grown to 13 clay and four hard courts. (Courtesy of the Greenville Country Club.)

TOURNAMENTS. The Greenville Country Club has hosted numerous golf tournaments throughout its history and continues to do so today. Seen here is Billy Delk, playing in the 1949 Club Championship. (Courtesy of the Greenville Country Club.)

COMPETITION. In the mid-1950s, Greenville leaders, including Alester G. Furman, Charles Daniel, and Francis Hipp, felt that the expanding local economy would support a new championship-grade golf course and club. Members of the Greenville Country Club shared this sentiment, and many worried their club would fall behind the new one, causing membership to drop. Green Valley Club did come to fruition, and the GCC felt its course needed to be renovated to remain competitive. (Courtesy of the Greenville Country Club.)

EXPANSION. Although the course had been renovated and expanded across the Reedy River to include seven new holes in 1962, four years later, the board of governors voted to have Heyward Sullivan approach course architect Robert Trent Jones to redesign the course yet again. After visiting the course, Trent Jones recommended building a completely new course. The GCC agreed and gave Jones seven plats of land as options for a new course, arriving upon the former Earle farm property just off Augusta Road as the most attractive option. In 1967, construction of the new course began and lasted two years. The name Chanticleer was adopted to coincide with the adjacent neighborhood. (Courtesy of the Greenville Country Club.)

CHANTICLEER. The course opened September 12, 1970, and was immediately held in high regard both locally and nationally. It was ranked as one of the Top 100 courses in the country by *Golf Digest* and rated in the top five most difficult courses in the state by the Carolinas Golf Association. (Courtesy of Hughes Development.)

CUP WORTHY. The Chanticleer course has hosted several tournaments, including a USGA National Open district qualifier, along with Carolina Golf Association and South Carolina Amateur events. In 1971, the club lobbied to have the 1975 Ryder Cup held at Chanticleer. Its work was thought to have been successful, but towards the end, Arnold Palmer spoke on behalf of his club, Laurel Valley, in Ligonier, Pennsylvania, and the USGA declared Laurel Valley as host. (Courtesy of Hughes Development.)

TORNADO. On a spring afternoon in March 1978, a volatile tornado touched down in the Chanticleer neighborhood and golf course. Homes and fairways suffered insurmountable damage. Over 3,000 trees were uprooted. (Both, courtesy of Hughes Development.)

DISCOVER THOUSANDS OF LOCAL HISTORY BOOKS FEATURING MILLIONS OF VINTAGE IMAGES

Arcadia Publishing, the leading local history publisher in the United States, is committed to making history accessible and meaningful through publishing books that celebrate and preserve the heritage of America's people and places.

Find more books like this at
www.arcadiapublishing.com

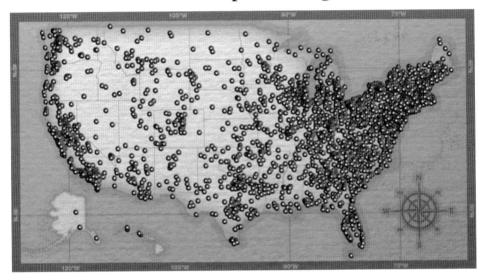

Search for your hometown history, your old stomping grounds, and even your favorite sports team.